THE FERAL CONDITION

THE FERAL CONDITION

POEMS

Gaylord Brewer

Negative Capability PRESS
MOBILE, ALABAMA

Cover Design by Natalie Young
Interior Design by Jordan Knox
Author Photo by John Guider

Library of Congress Control Number: 2018910601

ISBN: 978-0-94254-440-4

Negative Capability Press
62 Ridgelawn Drive East
Mobile, Alabama 36608
(251) 591-2922

www.negativecapabilitypress.org

Acknowledgments

These poems were written during returns to the Julia and David White Artists' Colony, Costa Rica, Decembers 2010 and 2014; the Centre d'Art i Natura in the Catalonian Pyrenees, Junes 2014 and 2015; and a first stay at ARTErra in rural Portugal during the summer of 2013. Respectively: In Ciudad Colón, Francisco resided in the big house. The views in Farerra still astounded, and—good luck for me—Lluís and Cesca (and Arnau) remained. For the best snails in Tondela, trust Micaela and João. Thanks to all for their kindness, thoughtfulness, and, of course, tolerance. There's likely no going back, but I'm grateful to have been there when it happened. Any other poems were composed out at the house in Tennessee between 2009–2012 (except for the prefatory poem, from 2016) and constitute the best of the non-"Ghost"—flora and fauna emphasized—attempts during that stretch. So, the geography's scattered.

Alimentum: "Field Report"

Asheville Poetry Review: "More Honored in the Breach: The Long Departure," "Squid"

Atlanta Review: "Ode to the Leaf-Cutting Ants of Costa Rica," "Three Feral Black Kittens, with a Modification to My Emerging Thesis," "Youth and Age"

Big Muddy: "Notation on the Last Light of the Year"

Briar Cliff Review: "At Last" (as "Last Man Standing"), "Iguana," "More Honored in the Breach: Talking to Your Dog on Skype," "Residence Rescinded," "Writing Spider"

Carolina Quarterly: "Little Gray Bird," "Longhorn Beetle," "The Natural World"

Cutthroat: "The Sea's Argument and After"

Epoch: "I Gently Chastise Sweeney on the Hyperbole Regarding His Battlefield Prowess," "Owl"

Evansville Review: "Corn Snake, or Red Rat Snake, Constrictor of the Genus Elaphe, Nocturnal, Harmless"

Georgia Review: "It Doesn't Matter If You're Careful"

Hawai'i Pacific Review: "Seasonal"

The Kerf: "More Honored in the Breach: Violating the Unhatched Eggs in the Compost Bin"

Lindenwood Review: "Caduceus"

Louisville Review: "Last Wild Iris Poem"

Natural Bridge: "More Honored in the Breach: A Note to Ghost, Absent"

Number One: "The Natural World," "The Natural World, Part Two"

The Pinch: "Sometimes, When You're Not Looking," "Turkey Vulture"

Rhino: "More Honored in the Breach: Last Sunday Afternoon Before You Leave a Good Place to which You'll Never Return"

River Styx: "All You Need to Bring"

Southern Poetry Anthology: Tennessee: "Interruption: A Coyote in Tennessee," "When I'm Gone"

Skylight 47 (Ireland): "Owl," "Pyrenees Wild Iris," "The Route of Santa Magdalena"

Sugar House Review: "Barred Falcon," "Cesca Explains the Flowers She Has Potted for My Balcony," "Overnight at Manuel Antonio," "The Route of Santa Magdalena"

The earth is mostly just a boneyard.
But pretty in the sunlight.

—*Larry McMurtry*

Contents

III: Bestiary, Tennessee

IV: Bestiary, Costa Rica

At Last

A single frantic bat
    cedes the night
        to chittering silhouette

of young owls.
    The savaging continues.
        By morning, grass

will shiver, tufts of blood-fur
    and stakes of bone
        frail as toothpicks.

I watch without resource
    or judgment, as I have
        for all my brief eternity—

before you were lost,
    before the others were lost.
        Before the pendulum

stopped dead on its scaffold.
    The commuted days—
        or decades, or centuries—

extinguished always
    to darkness and then
        warm light again

glistening on the carnage.
    I would try to explain,
        if there were anything

to explain, if there
    had been, if you were
        here to listen, or turn away.

I: Bestiary, Portugal

> Ay, marry, is't,
> But to my mind, though I am native here
> And to the manner born, it is a custom
> More honor'd in the breach than the observance.
>
> *—Hamlet*

More Honored in the Breach:
A Note to Ghost, Absent

Your kind of morning, Ghost:
the sun smothered by gray shroud
of sky, fields surrendered, this entire
house moaning its existence,
a spitting rain that seemed, somehow,

cruelly arbitrary. The kind of morning
to lie on a hard bed, pull the gloom
to your neck, try like hell not to remember.
I wasn't surprised you weren't here
when I arrived, not in the stone alleys,

not in the shadows of the forest,
not trembling, arms spread, among
the ravens and terraced vines. Perhaps
you tired of waiting for me, as in
the living world they have tired of my leaving.

But I don't believe so. Something happened
in the old church that night—its door
unlocked only once—when I stumbled,
spilling the wine, and the torch went out,
something I will never comprehend,

as only you could explain. I wouldn't say
I miss you, Ghost, or that the quiet
isn't welcome relief, but the intimacy
of our time . . . well. If I leaned
across the balcony last night, if I

accused unfairly, hopelessly conjuring
through the crystal of my glass, let's
call it nostalgia, a name no more wrong
than many we settled on. Ah, remember
the nightmare visits, the wounds,

always wounds? Remember when any bath
was a drowning, each feast rancid,
every bitch's bone a mocking skull?
Only I, and the cats of those countries,
saw you turning away. How could I help

feeling chosen, to watch you destroy
what you cherished and help draw
its name in ashes, transcribe each blessing
bruised and withered by your touch?
Remember when the sunset—so unlike

last night's—was blood augury
of the dark to follow and every howl
a song for ciphering? As I have written
these lines, the shroud has been pulled back.
The day's all blue skies now, all birdsong,

future, dreary promise. I am almost
grateful that you are not here to bear it.

More Honored in the Breach:
The Spider, Displaced

I brush away a new web,
fine and unruly, with the edge
of my book, and the spider
appears and disappears
beneath the arm of the chair.
I desire neither to kill
nor to be bitten, but this
is where I sit each morning
as I reflect on the night defeated
and the failed day ahead.
Soon, I am pondering
the crows and magpies
of the lost west, and the spider
is forgotten until I feel
a faint, persistent prick
on the hairs of my forearm.
And there she is—small, angular,
color of sand. I am certain
attention has been demanded,
though meaning eludes me.
I move my hand toward her
and she drops gracefully,
unharmed, to the marble below.
What then is this thing inside,
that breathes with my lungs,
pulses with my blood?
What awful blessing denied
and nourished for decades,
that I obey without fault, that
cannot be quelled or silenced?

More Honored in the Breach: Violating the Unhatched Eggs in the Compost Bin

The blond oval, balanced—
too heavy—in my hand,
then cracked, as gently as one may
crack an egg, among discarded
others, as if my intent were
to cook the sad contents
on its grave of dung. Smears
of blood and yolk slick my fingers.
I trace once this limp, gray thing
I've exposed. Soft beak, curl
of talon barely discernible.
But never to be in this world.
How far you came, little
chick, how close to emergence.

More Honored in the Breach:
Last Sunday Afternoon Before You Leave
a Good Place to which You'll Never Return

The sky still tender from night's berating
wind, the gate slouched from the beating
it took and didn't deserve. That sort of thing.
Church bell stupidly determined on
the lengthening hours, and the chickens,
who strut the same on Sunday as every other,
whose scripture is food—hard bread, soft cabbage,
broken corn if they can get it.

No nod to the world's depredations,
no exhausting despair, nothing at all, not here,
of the calamity of love. No quick gestures
with the hands. Maybe just a single
image of a woman unmoving on a swing,
the headlights of a car that may never arrive.
Maybe a spell of wildflowers, tentatively identified
from the pocket where they died:
spotted rockrose, dusky dog-fennel, sage.
Pimpernel, cistus, and marigold.
But too you could have all the names wrong,
so maybe not even that, not even.

More Honored in the Breach: Talking to Your Dog on Skype

I thought it would be fun, even funny,
and so at my insistence
my wife set her laptop on the carpet.
I missed seeing my girl, see, that's
the simple excuse, had heard her

growling out of sight of conversation.
On the blurry screen she looked
thin, out of proportion, but more
than that, I thought, *how small.*
Already I regretted this latest bad idea

on my list. I'm sorry, Lucy.
I don't know what voice you heard
as you retreated, ears back, head down,
and I persisted, high-pitched
and a little frantic, in our ritual phrases—

girlie, are you being good? taking care
of mommy? remember, you're in charge!—
what distorted face you saw, if any,
as your barking grew furious
at the wrongness of the thing

before you. I'd no way to undo what I'd
done as she ran moaning from the room,
no power to end the confusion
of this uncertain creature I vowed
to protect for all her years,

to care for and do no harm. Claudia,
close the screen. You were right,
of course. Lucy, there's a photo here—
you are smiling, posed, eyes shining
toward the green day beyond

the frame. Your heart-shaped tag
glows in the sun, and your daddy
is right there, where he's supposed to be,
speaking to you of your great beauty.

More Honored in the Breach:
Eating the Rabbit's Head,
Then Again Meditating upon the Subject

The rabbit dinner a rowdy déjà vu
of drink and appetite, ideas, jokes poorly
translated. Days following, no one

discovered my odd package in the freezer's
corner. Nobody cared, nobody
asked. Cared for what? Asked of what?

Alone in the house, I roasted
the head in a small ceramic dish,
a pretty blue one, simply: salt, pepper,

olive oil. Were these proper proportions?
Then, at the quiet table, a mystery
still unto myself, with my hands

I parted small teeth and ate its tongue,
for speech and desire; swallowed
both opalescent eyes, for failing vision;

broke the skull between thumbs
and scraped from within a nail's worth
of warm, rich brain, as if for understanding.

More Honored in the Breach:
The Long Departure

If I told you that man there, paused
out of sight of the crone singing
like an angel to her rows
of green corn, that he believes in his bones
he's Archangel of the Last God Standing,
the Great Deity of Faithlessness,
you wouldn't believe a word. You shouldn't.
I can testify, though, one morning he woke
and his beard was white, the taste of ash
soured his mouth and the gospel of futility
was his own. Follow as he approaches
a last time the dark men congregated
in the door of the village bar. It is his
final morning among them, and he offers each
a silent blessing none will notice,
crosses the sheared flocks of the field,
crosses the stupid animals of the courtyard who
copulate in their own shit. In ten minutes, believe me
or not, no matter, church bells will shudder
under the awful new hour. Our holy man will be gone.
He had prophesied that the sun would rage
red and full for his passage, and thus
the cold clouds of heaven descended.
I tell you, such is his terrible power.

II: Bestiary, Catalonia

They notice how his persona has changed,
having seemed himself to have taken on the
characteristics of an itinerant pedlar of old,
a vendor of gauds, a man leaning on a staff,
quavering, a bearer of strange knowledge.

—*Eoin McNamee*

The Route of Santa Magdalena

Come from Andorra in the east,
    or south across the *coll*—the throat—
    del Grau where it opens. Come
    from the north, between the *bordes*
    of la Plana and de Llosar,
    where neither cattle nor grass remain.

Come by the punishing west road,
    through stand of oak, fir,
    pine and ash, the small rare juniper,
    from Burg, Farrera, Alendo.
    Come from the south, over Castellarnau,
    said to be impassable, across

the river Lot, via the Pass of Sound.
    Arrive by foot, or as you will,
    the gliding wings of a lone vulture,
    muscled and wide, as compass.
    Arrive with the clothes on your back,
    blade for rending, package of salt

for wounds. As offering,
    kerchief stained of tears and sweat.
    If the chapel door opens, know
    that your audience is now, that she waits
    here as she has for twelve hundred
    years, patient in her sorrow.

Crucifix extended in one delicate
    grasp, skull the other—you may
    touch either. Approach her in this place
    of shadows. She hears all languages.
    On the altar, a chaos of needs,
    hundreds from as many hands,

the sheets torn, creased,
    faded and bled. From your own
    pocket bring the words you penned—

prayer for who remains, prayer
for release from the dark thing
that holds you—to shuffle with the rest.

Too soon, the impossible return
to wherever you left. If you believed,
she might give you strength.

The Woman

I was returning down the mountain,
arguing aloud with myself about
my life. Storm rising dark and fast
from the south. I don't know what
moment she appeared on the outcropping.
White hair and dress conversant
with wind, wicker basket in crook of arm.
Ethereal is the word I thought then
but didn't speak, and I hoped she would
let me pass so I needn't announce my ignorance.
But she watched as I approached,
greeted me. I believe now she read
easily my foreignness, that I was marked.
A storm imminent, that much I knew.
We waited in the narrowing space.
I indicated roiling sky, gestured insensibly
toward her full basket of elderberry flowers.
The sharp wrinkles of eyes and mouth
beautiful. Her leathered face beautiful.
I unclasped my pack, confessed
the berries I had foraged, the handful
of wild rosebuds cut for a vase. Don't ask why.
From above, she nodded to a bloom-
heavy rose climbing a wall of the village,
its season nearly finished. Wind coming
faster, colder, full certainty, carrying darkness.
I looked where she pointed,
then back as she raised palm to face
and inhaled a fierce, imagined fragrance.

Exiled from My Room on Cleaning Day,
I Pass a Sympathetic Hour with Sweeney

Perhaps not the exacted bird-curse
of Ronan, cleric you assaulted, but Anna
the housekeeper does take her time.
Perhaps, Sweeney, not rending branch

of blackthorn where you perch, bloodied,
but still drafty where I sit here alone—
stiff chair, thin blanket, cold calves exposed.
As we haunt the moors and loughs

together, avian ghosts to the battlefield
of your defeat, perhaps we do not mate,
quite, like "hard-shanked cranes,"
but I acknowledge your tempestuous flights,

ravaged years as wanderer, longing
and disdain always intertwined.
Your preference for the blackbird's song
and wind across scourged landscape.

After each grim night or close escape
you "speak your poem"—with a cost, yes,
but as naturally as breath and without
concern of praise. Pale aspen or oak rod

"to and fro," yew tree in the dark churchyard,
your beloved bellowing stag—these
are Sweeney's audience. But let us pause.
Here, balanced in a modest corner of

our exile, Anna's wicker basket of conjuring:
her totems of grass, bark, and cone;
her potions for sale: unguents and *pomadas*,
herb sachets and oils of *roses*, *lavandra*,

camamilla, romaní, sweet-scented
and soothing seductions, mad friend,
with a high price. I will soon reclaim
the luxuries of the four walls where I rule:

floor swept and mopped, rugs beaten,
soft sheets tucked, thick towel to dry
my cleansed body. I will leave you, for now,
to your crazed and riven places, verses

of little solace. A last cool sip at cherished
Glen Bolcain, a bite of watercress
and sorrow, cold comforts to sustain us.
It just makes sense we've found each other

at last. Or maybe you were waiting
by the old gate, at edge of sight, all along.

Cesca Explains the Flowers
She Has Potted for My Balcony

By the second rapid-fire
    insistence, brushing jagged
leaves with fingertips,
    that this one, that has no name,

lives forever, I realize the phrase
    is not a mythic reference,
but that this nameless one,
    which will throw out

the tentacles of its blooms,
    is perennial. The thick knot
of small pink petals,
    clavell, which I recognize as dianthus,

too lives forever. And there,
    humble beneath, the one you find,
always, in cemeteries.
    And *thees one*—caressing

the willowy fronds—this one will
    rise up strong in a single
beautiful flower. Blue,
    we think. And here, the last—

sanguine trumpets
    drooped and shivering,
She die in the winter in the mountains.
    What, I ask?, startled again

by the force of the narrative.
    Who died? We struggle together
for a moment to resurrect
    a name. Petunia! Ah!

Who dies in the winter
    in the mountains. Of course.
Who does not live forever.

Three Feral Black Kittens, with a Modification to My Emerging Thesis

For days I have been note-taking
for my opus chastising the poets
for their cat poems. But as I ease shut
the lock on an afternoon expedition
trespassing Casa Ramón—
revealed in the future—the first
black lump, fleeing up stone steps
with a faint, half-hearted meow,
surprises me, then a second in retreat.
The third—glowing emerald eyes,
patchy fur—holds squeezed ground
beneath a slate stoop, hissing
with all the high-pitched kitten ferocity
it can muster, teeny red maw
stretched wide, teeny pointed teeth,
a display of hatred and fear laudable
for one so little. No mother's tit,
no shelter from the week's cold rain.

When I return with two deep jar lids,
carton of milk, tin of chicken
and liver cat food—to be explained
in my exposé—I find the runts
in a dark, dank gap of rubble
between uninhabited houses.
Out of human reach, anyway.
One, possibly Badass, watches me.
One climbs. One, lost in that gloom.
I pour milk, finger out gelatinous
pâté, place both lids on a flat log,
foolish I will be exposed. But kittens,
I decide then and there—I've
been weighing this—are exempt
from all diatribe, and maybe
even deserve an occasional verse.
Especially the hissing, shivering ones,
with green eyes and nowhere to go.

Pyrenees Wild Iris

This entire month I've searched
the meadows for them,
a confirmation of time
and memory. Twelve years spent.
Then, in the final days,
a cluster of buds in a ravine.

I should have let them be
and done no harm, but I couldn't
help myself, could not:
I had to have them. I cut five
with my knife, wrapped
their wounds in a cloth wetted

in the stream. I've no taxonomy
to describe the reaching
upper petals, languorous tongues
of lower striped with yellow.
The intensity of the violet,
the orchid-like delicacy.

Suffice to say, they have opened
quickly in water, given
their slayer two days of happiness.
Now, on the third, I depart
and am unlikely to return. It is Sunday.
Nothing further is required.

The closet hangs empty, the bed
is stripped. The table, too,
is bare, except for this note
and a small glass of five wild iris
at the peak of their brief perfection,
which I leave for you.

Little Gray Bird

Or crag martin, as I learned
this morning, when
I woke thinking of you,
only then to confirm you
are gregarious out of mating season
and, though sometimes victim
to the hunger of crows,

of stable population.
That was later. We had shared
our moment, the mountains
radiant with sunset,
you arched on the stone wall.
My full attention:
the black needle of your beak,

twiggy legs on which you
raised and lowered emphatically,
then wagged tail feathers.
Lately, yes, I am prone
to moods and emotions
but knew whom these gestures
were for. You studied

me with the dark dot of your
eye, repeated the dance.
It had been a doubtful
day. You seemed to sense
this, or perhaps we were both
merely anxious for our supper.
But for one full minute,

before you shat—suddenly,
as if to settle the matter—
shook again and took veering flight,
our worlds focused on
each other, what you were trying
so urgently to tell me
that I needed to know.

Longhorn Beetle

Already that morning, I had moved my slipper
as not to injure a firebug, *pyrrhocoris apterus*,
come to visit in sporty red jetpacks of abdomen.
But it was the beetle that unnerved me,

brought me onto elbows and knees, backside
to the village chapel, ridge of pine, snow-streaked
alps in uncontainable distance. The longhorn's
black antennae were, as you would imagine,

exquisite, twice the length of its body,
sleek and seeking mustachios from a Dalí dream.
I couldn't help prodding with a fingertip.
Each time the head lowered in four quick gestures,

the thorax throbbed, and if I bent my ear
to within a vulnerable inch, four tiny squeaks
of reproach from an alien world. This is no
ars poetica, friend, no naturalist guide, no tale

of romance or transformation. But it was Sunday,
after all, and I was on my knees, bowed
in close attention. On closed wings,
a dusting of gold, images too miniscule

to read in text untranslatable. I don't know
why it stayed, allowed me to pursue my game.
Finger push, four nods, four tiny sustained squeaks—
punctuated, terrifying. Monster in miniature.

But as it studied this colossal pixilated shape
through compound eyes, snapped teeny mandibles
with a wishful clack against giant nail,
and the beautiful head lowered once, twice,

three times, four, squeak, squeak, squeak, squeak,
you would have required no poet or coleopterist,
no semiologist or lover, to understand
exactly the suggestion being offered.

Monday Morning Cat

Her cry is mournful,
a trill of need and sadness
that pulls me again
from the page of my book.
I search the slanted rooftops
below, the stone path,
lean as far over balcony
as I dare to listen hard

among broken walls
and wild tangles of branch,
around obscuring edges
of marigold and geranium
newly potted and hung.
Hail summer, welcome!
On the farthest promontory,
cold scars of snow

half or less their size of
two weeks ago. The peaks
of middle distance greening.
She begins again her ragged
purring plea, invisible,
resonant from one place,
then another, as if haunting
spirit of cat or cat deception.

The hidden stream,
boisterous behind tree line.
The cuckoo, dull and constant,
never knowing the time
for silence. And this quiet
wanting that only I hear,
inhuman, meant for me or not,
that I cannot answer,

wounded call toward whatever
the next days will bring.

I Gently Chastise Sweeney
on the Hyperbole Regarding
His Battlefield Prowess

> I left him shortened by a head
> and left the torso, overjoyed,
> and left five other princes dead
> before I stopped to wipe my blade.
>
> —from *Sweeney Astray*, trans. Seamus Heaney

Sweeney, I know that time is the great foe
in wilderness, know from the distance
of a lost life the allure of telling the tale
as it might have, should have, could have . . .
I, too, fill hours with my indignant and
animated voice, in converse with deaf forest
and the rutted, dung-littered path.
I also sip the cold stream and announce it
all that remains of the holy. I am the one
ear in the world this morn bent to your woe.

But Sweeney, *sweetie*, you haven't leveled
any goliaths lately, and beserker Oilill might
as well never have advanced in mighty strides
for all the kids in this town give a shit.
And no need to *talk* it if you can *do* it, ya know?
Yes, "shortened by a head" is a clever turn,
and yes we're both romantics in love
for the keen phrase, the hook, the pizzazz.
Maybe that's our problem. Wandering glens
and passes, reciting to the wind, why not?
But from the bloody field of Moira
to the rock face of my mountain with its façade
of greenery, nobody's bringing home any
trophy heads anymore. Alright, Sweeney,
have it your mad and merry way, what solace
you can muster from bitter revision.
One bit of advice you already know:

Careful when you clean the blade and crow
over body count. When your guard's down,
when the spear you never saw coming—
lucky throw by some dim local yokel
with a hard-on for you—tears the dream apart.

This Is the Day

To defer all movement.
Still hands.
No human speech

is justified. Breathe silence.
A vibration
of violin, faint and wistful—

village requiem.
Rain overwhelms
the song. Fog presses firmly,

its immutable art
of obliterating the world.
Today,

decide nothing,
have no opinion on your life.
What you've done

or what you failed to do.
Take solace
in the thought of the mountains—

forest of birch, black oak,
trumpet of wild gentian,
rhododendron set to burst,

red profusion
offered only to the hermit, mad,
to the faithless gypsy

or to no one.
Time suffocates
between sky and earth.

You are no part of this.
You are part of this.

Exquisite Human Suffering

The fish woman hoses the gore
from her slab, slaps another carcass onto
marble and resumes precise knife work.
Displayed on ice, a single lobster
twitches a leg. Drooping antenna
shifts a fraction, one bulbous eye rotates.
It's unrestricted but going nowhere
under the fluorescents and measuring gaze
except to the boiling sea of pain its destiny,
butter and a squirt of lemon.
At that price, though, the slow freezing,
the suffocation will meanwhile continue.

Let's ignore the routine hell of flies
haloing the donkey's nostrils and mouth.
They're not pretty, and do we not seek
the picturesque, a narrative of consolation?
Let us confide, as if to a dull child,
an admiration for her fine, sculpted ears.
But where the bridle sores the cheek,
layers of complacent flies ruin our scene.
A crawling poultice of suffering, undeterred
in the savor of flesh. Meanwhile,
the jenny's dark eye searches, finds us
wanting. No further comment regarding ears
or the sweet summer grass's abundance.

This, the world in its awful beauty.
On our nature hike, we wistfully misname
one plucked blossom after another.
Poked with walking stick, the ants rush
from their cities of dung, a fascinating
and complex society. We crush hundreds,
whole generations, without even trying.
Unavoidable, if we're to continue on the trail.
What choice but that the big lives stomp
the small? There, just ahead, a spotted fawn
shoulder-high in mountain clover!
A goldfinch greets with melancholy song!
Meanwhile, every step another bloodbath.

Caduceus

. . . it was often depicted being carried in
the left hand of Mercury, the messenger of
the gods, guide of the dead and protector
of merchants, shepherds, liars, and thieves.

They spring from nowhere, it seems,
fast, agile, foot or more straight upward,
entwined in coitus, battle, or play.
Serps verd-i-groga, olive-and-yellow
snakes, though in the assault
of afternoon sun they look black, slashed
with glowing color. They see you
and drop. Slithering flash of skin,
quick *shush* through grass, vanished
into the scree. How to witness
such a thing, symbol alive and writhing?

You toe the weeds a bit. Then, alone on
the pitiless descent to Tírvia, too late
an hour to have begun such folly,
grip walking stick by crook of handle,
plant it on the twisted road, and go.

A Little Sunday Poem

The shapely linden
risen from stone
by the bolted door
of the Chapel of St. Roch,
beneath its silent bell—
nascent bloom,
palms of up-turned leaves
glowing in the sun.

Barn swallows
plunging
and looping—dark, tireless
blades of flight,
of seeming joy.

A faint and languid
barking,
one plaintive rooster,
bee buzzing windowpane—
otherwise, the village
so quiet
it could be deserted
of everyone but you.

Old German Shepherd

Less bark now than moaning cough—
faintly, infrequently offered out
to the world, just to stay
in the game. No attempt at standing.

Any shift on the vinyl cushion—
efficient for hosing away
incontinence—is a shift of pain.
Bucket of water, bowl. No toys.

When I whisper down, *hey, buddy,*
the erect ears acknowledge nothing.
Pastor Alemán, phrase recently
learned I thought clever.

Between my balcony bars,
a panting grin. I watch him
watch the night gather—slowly, then
suddenly—until his pretty owner,

a rare single woman in the village,
appears, rubs the gray head,
adjusts harness of rope around
bony hips, and helps her animal limp

into their home, the day finished.

Last Wild Iris Poem

This was no serendipity,
no surprise and feigned hesitance.
This was tactical extraction—

surgical, considered.
Today, there would be no
talk of "orchid-like delicacy"

or "languorous tongues of petals,"
no coy labial nonsense
or conceit of a perfection

I guiltily leave
behind. Thirteen years ago,
these fields common

with bloom by June's end.
Now, as I depart a third
and final time, nothing to chance.

Scissors for cutting, cloth
to wet in the stream
and wrap amputated stems.

At 2000 meters, sun a hammer,
flies at eyes and ears, bare-ankle
deep in ants marching

their theatre of war,
I would have the iris again
and close this story. I'd never

hiked so far, climbed
as treacherously (with scissors),
but long in the afternoon,

descent and night ahead,
I find six specimens in fair mid-bloom
—the last in this meadow,

perhaps in all the Pyrenees—
bend each thick scape
to the blade, and take them.

Owl

I have deserved all this:
night-vigils, terror . . .
women's cried-out eyes.

—from *Sweeney Astray*, trans. Seamus Heaney

For nights you beckoned me—
your chittering whispers, sharp cries.
So close, as if from balcony
beyond the shut doors.
Each time I stepped out squinting
and naked, I saw darkness.
Then last night, 3:00 a.m.,
legs aching, I left that room
and followed hallway to empty studio.
How could you have sensed me
entering that shadowed space, *how*?
The flitting peripheral flight,
then perched on the apex of the roof
your huge, impossible shape
glowing in the half-moon,
the great muscled shoulders,
and I stopped, humbled and ashamed,
sensed all of my life folded
in your merciless wings,
and I did not know, however it may
sound, whether morning would
return, or if this was my fate,
this cavernous room, pale streetlight,
your suddenly turned head
and the luminous, baleful eyes:
*Foolish man. You know nothing
of the wild world. Go from this place.
Go home, if you've yet one to go to.*

III: Bestiary, Tennessee

Jefe: I have no wish to paint the world in colors more somber than those it wears, but as the world gives way to darkness it becomes more and more difficult to dismiss the understanding that the world is in fact oneself. It is a thing which you have created, no more, no less. And when you cease to be so will the world. There will be other worlds. Of course. But they are the worlds of other men and your understanding of them was never more than an illusion anyway. Your world—the only one that matters—will be gone.

—*Cormac McCarthy*

Writing Spider

For who would not admire your
beauty, yellow brocade of abdomen—
a Rorschach—eight black stockings
on thin legs? Your radial silks

marking my wife's wild garden—
grapevine, sedum, angelonia.
Conjure-words. Even invasion
so near our door I accepted as prophecy.

I'd heard the stories of your talent.
Weeks passed. You spun fly, beetle,
wasp into sticky whiteness,
round and round in patient claws.

Remains of a devoured mate,
so small as if your child, hung limply
for a day. I felt our evening arrive.
Beneath glowing trumpets

of moonflower, then, I came close—
breathed my name three times,
then the fatal forth across your design.
Spin me in the text of your hunger,

record my doom with the cruel stylus
of your body. Next morning,
stabilimentum looked the same
harsh zigzag. Symbol or encryption,

gibberish to me. Though the anchor
strands, I admit, surprised—
how strong, resistant as I tore
each loose, destroyed every trace.

Squid

Their cavities I fatten with feta cheese,
chopped black olive, Italian parsley,
lemon juice, olive oil, black and hot pepper.
The opaque tubes are slippery,
open ends flopping, so I abandon

my spoon and enact the whole mess
with fingers, massaging each length
to stuff it plump throughout. Then pucker
shut and suture with a wood skewer.
Thus, a half hour and more is killed,

buried with activity, and I move on to
whatever I may concoct for the next murder.
Later, I will blacken these odd creatures
on the grill, serve with roasted lemons,
sea salt, another drizzle of good oil.

By then I'll be drunk, my wife and I
fighting or not fighting, another day
mortgaged to darkness in a summer barely
begun. When this one's over, one fewer
will remain. I'll drink the wine, eat

the hot, charred bodies with my hands,
await the owls who come at evening.
I will butcher their purrs and soft trills
as the dark ones marvel at my distorted aria,
the rituals and long shadows of our table.

Seasonal

First, harbingers of forsythia and crocus.
We've survived again. Quickly now
fields of daffodil. We're stunned into April—

tulip, hyacinth, lilac, columbine and cherry.
These the sounds we incant. Yes,
each blooms and dies away. But May,

if you remain, will yield rose and iris,
foxglove, veronica, first scapes of the lilies
that rule June. When these rise in profusion,

we can, if you agree, each morning
stand among them, count and welcome
by name the new bouquet, break away

pallid flowers of the day before, a day
forever ended. June, eh? If skepticism remains,
consider hydrangea, French and Spanish

lavender, nocturnal veil of moonflower.
All is not lost or ceded. Much persists.
Even the hard truth of July has its lures—

crepe myrtle, enduring herb. Say with me
as if you believe—rosemary and mint,
tarragon, thyme, oregano, chive. See

where this is going? Yes, the procession
arrives then withers, our finest season ever
or not quite what we'd dreamed, all whether

you stay or go, as well known by custom.
Do as you will. The garden tends its own life,
defiant beneath the scythe of August.

Youth and Age

Let them have the fashionable
cloak of sorrow, its dark fabric too heavy
for the sun. Leave them
despair rendered for the stage
and the phrased anger of protest.
Leave them the nights.
They can have, too, the papers
consigned to trash—conceits
abandoned, the urgent list of tasks
not undertaken, the sack of mail unsorted,
the new news unread.
Let them have the Next Essential Thing
and the noise it carries.
You'll keep silence, keep the morning,
keep the parchment of hours
that charts the sky. You'll keep
the Inca dove, the postman butterfly,
the Passion of Christ flower
bloomed red by the waterside for one day only.
Keep the whiskered dog, otherwise
still, who slaps its gray tail once, twice,
thrice to announce
it too still lives and too is nameless.
Keep in your percussive heart
their contempt at your antiquation,
the priceless gift of dismissal.
Keep greedily the groans
of the body that register you're here,
the body you've settled into for a lifetime.
The shoulder that freights
a box of simple goods
up the hill, the hand that grips the key
to swing the gate,
the legs that step stubbornly forward
rather than dance in circles.

The Natural World

What did I see? Too many wings and beaks,
an agitation, a violence. Screeching brought me
to the window. When the just-hatched chick
flung from the box I witnessed the horror
but couldn't name it. I started running anyway.
Unlocked deadbolt, leapt yelling-clapping

into shaggy clover. By then, three others curled
by the pole, bald heads limp on distended necks,
unfledged wings, bulging eyes never to open.
The chickadee parents frantic in the trees,
darting and calling, sparrow marauders silent,
watchful. Christ, how I yearned to kill them,

crush those preening lives in my fist. I regretted
returning my father's rifle, longed for the carnage
I could bring, the sweet, too-late retribution.
Instead, I raised each twitching corpse
no larger than thumbnail, unlatched the door
of the house I, myself, had installed, and lay

bodies in the mossy nest now a grave. For hours,
endless, the chatter outside screen—their loss
and anger, their denial. I closed the window
and left. In the morning, a single still shape
remained. I pulled loose the whole mess,
pointlessly gentle, and carried it to the woods.

The Natural World, Part Two

Whom was I kidding? I watched raging
and helpless as the sparrows ravaged
chickadees in the box, tossed the clutch
to the ground by their necks. Righteousness
secure, I wrote the stanzas to get full
credit. Then that same afternoon—
same doorbell, yes, where vespid had stung
my allergic wife as dinner guests arrived,
my vindication and argument secure
from a year before—I rang the clapper
again and again, viciously, corroded iron
heaving as if in storm, until the dark
other dropped from the waist of the bell.
I severed the modest hive, held it in sunlight—
six alien shapes, aqueous, just moving—
ripped from their beginning. So what?
I tossed the nest, wiped my hand clean.
Turning, I watched the mother writhe
on wings in the black mulch of our garden.
It took three grindings of sandal to end
her pain, deliver the full weight of mercy.

Corn Snake, or Red Rat Snake, Constrictor of the Genus Elaphe, Nocturnal, Harmless

The scales cool in my grip,
smooth body taut and strong.
I went for the male first, into the box,
then the writhing and resistant
female, too quick for my first pass.
Yes, their cozy daily return beneath
the gutter pipe uneased me, even after
my wife's cries of copperhead
were quieted. They looked too much
at home; breeding season had begun.
I didn't share my father's bloodlust
for any and all, but I feared them.
I knelt there, admired hypnotic
patterns, darker intricacies of the male,
its tail raised and faintly rattling,
fawn mate a shade of sand, the coil
of her as my hand closed on them.

Interruption: A Coyote in Tennessee

A scream began it. I was at the door
in seconds. Along perimeter of woods,
she limped our lawn as we gawked.
Small across brutal evening, coat
darkly silver. Doggedly to somewhere.
I'd sighted one in the drive a decade ago

through headlights and fog, a story
no one believed. What choice now?
I snagged binoculars and followed
down that same gravel path. Followed
across our mowed field, toward
the trafficked highway. For a moment lost

in wild fescue the county had let go,
she appeared, tentative at edge
of pavement. A truck with black windows
had pulled aside twenty feet ahead,
waiting. As she peered across two lanes
toward what was there, I focused—

snout, taut ears, tail. Ashen fur.
Dark eyes. *If you're determined to cross,*
damn it, then cross. Cross now if you will.
The pick-up growled. I lowered the glasses.
With balletic grace, she crossed.
Crossed white line, yellow, white.

Soundlessly crossed rippled heat,
beautiful hopeless moment, limping
past the barber's trailer, sharply east
for denser woods. A black window lowered.
Its fleshy face stared at me. "Red fox?"
When my wife screamed, I had been

deviling eggs, thinking vaguely
of my tired life, its trite yearnings.
The human face called out again

as I backed away. The limp worried me,
as did the future, and I wondered
what accident or attack sent her running.

Field Report

My wife lunches out with a friend
and the dog has hidden the uneaten
half of rawhide chew and now curls,
eyes closed, in a tattered chair
taken from my parents twenty years ago
or more. It's the dead-end of summer.
August has relented, just a bit.
You suggest I should let the day pass,
that I've nothing of merit to add
to the argument of war, what the fall
will bring, my own nightly failings?
Of course you're right. But why not
a few words of greeting this afternoon,
a quiet invitation? Gutters bulge
already, but they can wait. Tomorrow
I'll rebuild the rotted back stoop.
For now, let's speak of the moon
two nights before, raised satin head
of the moonflower, blowsy and glowing,
dog and I dozing on the porch
where I dozed with another a decade ago.
How it was: first seasons, then years,
then decades. I cut the greenest
basil this morning for a final batch
of pesto. As the leaves soaked,
spiders and dowsed insects crawled
to the highest tips of their sunk ship.
See, this is what I had to tell you.
Mince local garlic, grind Reggiano
and pepper. Pinch of sea salt and steady
drizzle of oil into the pulsing mush—
sexy, easy. Tonight we'll roast chicken,
slice last tomatoes of the year,
even go outside to admire the sharp
border the lawn boys carved yesterday.
Then listen again for the owls.
This is what I wanted you to know.
Maybe we'll get lucky. Maybe we were.

When I'm Gone

Front lights will still glow
across the porch I built, fail again
against the winter night.

Moon and stars will hang
sharply in determined positions
of gods and fortunes.

The dog, no longer young
but still painless in her joints,
will sit attentively

on earth on a loose leash,
accustomed to the house
down the road no longer new,

flickering mirage
that once so disturbed her peace.
She'll be dreaming of someone

else, awaiting someone else,
as will my wife—
this all as it should be.

More ornamental bones
in the frozen ground,
the world spinning toward
spring even as it seems so still.

Notation on the Last Light of the Year

Perhaps another hour, suffused behind
cloud on an ominously warm day turning
toward its night. Time to follow dog Lucy
for a few final feints and circles
in the mud and unconquerable leaves, time
for these simple and marginal notes.

Twelve months ago I prayed to the sky
for one more year, the comforting
cloak of status quo I cherish. When I wore it,
it didn't fit as it had, softness threadbare
and frayed. Pick your own senseless
symbol, friend, for the light is fading.

Time for a last lope, no coat required,
just to growl a bit and chase the ball beneath
our graying heaven. Time, just, to toast
our helpless hope, and your health, sir,
and the darkness into which the old passes,
the darkness from which the new begins.

IV: Bestiary, Costa Rica

Your heart is beating, isn't it?
You're not in chains, are you?

—*Mary Oliver*

All You Need to Bring

Our tested rule is this: Arrange
on the bed every item you believe
required, then prove the need of each.
Return, first, yellowed books
to their shelf. No hours will be orphaned
to leisure and you've solitary thoughts
for distraction. Remove
camera and field glasses—
there will be no recording,
no animal to remark in the darkness
of our temporary camp, a darkness
sufficient also to repel your pallid torch.
Put it away. Leave your treats
and water bottle, your squat
portion of drink. Your hunger will be
of a different sort, and we,
experienced in our trade, will
tend to it as we must. Your thirst, however,
you will find unquenchable, though you may
gulp deeply of the salt sea,
on your knees in its black tide
as we prepare the boats.
You will require no toiletries,
no soap, no comb, no razor,
no soft cloth to dry your face.
Vanities will be unnecessary,
indeed unwelcome, during your brief
residence among us. Remember
the importance of weight, that dimensions
are essential, and return all shirts
and slacks to their hangers,
all undergarments to drawers,
your hat to its hook. Close purse
and closet luggage on the shelf.
Your coins will have no worth,
jewels no luster. Only the rags
on your back and sandals roped to feet
may be bartered in the chill night.

Discard passport. You'll have no origin.
Bring no clock. Here, its hands
would still the moment you arrive.

Sometimes, When You're Not Looking

The world gives a gift
    it knows you need right away,
        say a squirrel scouting

a banana bunch hung to ripen.
    Not the scrawny rodent
        of where you grew up,

but squirrel with the plush
    auburn coat and long tail
        of monkey, handsome

animal amorous and wary.
    She watches, peel slack
        in her jaws, as you approach

and select a small
    fruit for yourself, strip away
        to its tower of soft flesh

and join her. Today,
    say, the sun you'd waited for
        arrived, hot and clear,

the coinage of your afternoon
    spent swimming, exposing
        pale skin of chest and legs

to a luxurious burn. Or
    when you stepped from the shower,
        walked naked and damp

to the window as if summonsed,
    there the toucan
        of rumor, upside down

in a slender, swaying tree.
    The one you'd sought for days
        without hope, silently

plucking green pods with
    the glowing scimitar of her beak,
      for only you to witness.

Barred Falcon

Trees glow after rain.
   As if cued the falcon
      arrives suddenly above me,

folds fan of gray wing.
   As if . . . expecting answers.
      It is not yet 9:00 a.m.

I've hardly had time to
   draw curtains, sweep the floor,
      or consider what shape

to assign the morning's pain.
   The bird turns implacable
      head, fluffs itself with a shiver,

cleans black tip of
   short, down-turned beak
      with talon, in no hurry.

Giving me time to consider.
   Tentatively, I study
      magnified chest feathers

in the breeze, unwavering
   yellow eye. At last, failed
      and patience spent, it

leans forward and opens silently
   into the sky. What can I do,
      with my blurry vision,

my foolish slippers slickly
   clomping over grass,
      but hurry after this inquisitor

who has arrested my day
   and found me wanting?
      As if to cry, *Wait!* Or,

Dark One, give me one chance more.

It Doesn't Matter If You're Careful

This is the morning
    to slow thoughts
        in rhythm to
            stillness. You can never

halt them while living.
    The heat
        you craved arrived.
            Now, a little rain

to cool things
    would be a blessing.
        Sit on this stoop,
            partly in shade, partly

dappled sun.
    As it has always been.
        Sit as long as you please,
            as if you shared

the world
    in its great tolerance.
        To take up just one's
            proper space,

and no more. But
    no less. Not to swagger,
        nor taunt. The wind
            in the bamboo

shushes every conceit.
    A breeze moves
        its fingertip along
            your leg, a white scar.

Edging the path,
    a profusion of
        purple blooms,
            perhaps the shade

of a wedding dress
    many years ago,
        a different century.
            Five tissues of petal,

dark narrow
    blades of leaves.
        Low click of locust,
            the kiskadee's shrill

warning.
    You can live
        a long time, if you listen,
            and you're lucky.

Mockingbird

Perhaps the hawk on a cold-eyed
   prowl, the crow feeling
      peckish, the goldfinch's joy

or neurotic energy of the wren.
   The owl's ghostly patrol.
      Don't forget the binge of buzzard,

its bellyful always a winner.
   Pick the birds you do best,
      steal with abandon, line your nest

with shiny baubles.
   Your choices will change
      as the decades rough your throat,

but go on. Belt it with conviction.
   Answer the birder's query
      with a querulous eye. Witness

only to your original song.
   Mimicry by morning, mimicry
      for noon, mimicry at midnight.

Mimicry Monday to Friday,
   north, south, east, west.
      Mimicry winter, spring, and fall,

rain, sleet, or shine.
   Mimicry all summer long.
      The warbling just distorted,

faintly tone-deaf, but convincing
   enough. No one's listening
      too carefully. Don't worry

over the derivative nature
   of your calling, that some day
      truth will clip your wings.

The trees are bowed with mockery,
   after all, a racket of pomp
      and plumage looking after its own.

Little Gray Gecko

How long had you watched me
before I noticed you there
blending into the windowsill?
From then, I couldn't help
looking up after each page,
looking up from portents
just received, to ensure you were
with me. Hardly an inch
including tail. Your tiny toe pads,
your bulbous eyes turned
in my direction. You seemed content,
accepting of the situation.
I would catch you
and take you outside before dark,
but no hurry. Alone here
with my book and bad news,
I appreciated the company.

So small, so swift—I feared
hurting you. You evaded brute
fingers, dropped, parried,
were coaxed into a coffee cup.
Your chirps surprised me.
But when I lay cup in the grass,
you weren't inclined
for freedom. Prompted,
you topped the rim, posed
on painted blue flowers.
To enticement of wounded ant,
you remained unmoved.

Finally, then, I forced you
in skittering starts over
the hard earth, and as I did
felt a surge of sadness,
an absurd heaviness of heart.
I thought my austere
rooms inhospitable for you.
Out here you looked too small

to exist. What had I done?
My charity? Dark was coming,
another punishing wind
gathering breath, as I stood
and entered the empty house.

Overnight at Manuel Antonio

1.

There is a price to pay
for a beach paradise,
not merely cramped hours
on bus or the cost
of entry. The price
of everything
outside the boundary,
every huckster and
very special deal, amigo.
Price of sleep, of security.
But as 12 years ago,
floating naked at 7:10 a.m.,
sharing sky only
with brown pelicans
and sand with hermit crabs,
warmth swaying
and holding me, I can
afford this and more.

2.

There is a price to pay
for a balcony seat
over orchestra of sea.
In wallet, tired legs.
I've it all to myself—
except a family of parrots;
one pair of aracaris
perched, considering;
a single shy agouti
sniffing out a snack of fruit.
Flamed horizon,
coast, cloud, sun
demand full attention.
For brief, infinite hour
I breathe each moment

without want or
complaint, until the world's
edge is dark again.

Costa Rica, Day Four without Internet

No CNN, no scores,
    update on market losses
    real-time or otherwise.
    Only the ceaseless creak—

a ship's straining hull—
    of bamboo, the quick
    company of hummingbirds.
    I am disgusted

at the soft thing I've become,
    typical creature of nervous
    and distracted times,
    eager to blame

a simpler culture.
    I tap out the days.
    Week's end. Expect
    nothing but the convocation

of sunset, the deepening oranges
    and azures behind
    this ring of black mountains,
    bats a blur of hunger.

I worry: my father's blood work,
    my wife and dog surrounded
    by a noose of workmen
    far past deadline.

Of the worry I'm causing.
    Days are easier
    if the weather's fair.
    Roaming the congestion

of the village,
    its dusty fruit stalls.
    The church bell without pattern.
    Yesterday, a funeral.

At night I have rum, chats
    with the dead, jungle calls.
    One thought is this:
    In four days more, likely

all will be restored. We'll
    boot up, exhale, chart
    every instant of lost time,
    laugh at baseless fears.

And when in my life
    will I ever again be
    off the map, perfectly alone
    with this verdant wildness?

Protégé

I guess the kid's got a big heart
    and means well, but he hits the tent
like God's Lone Conscript—
    urgent, unwashed, red as a cherry,

three days chasing his ass in the jungle.
    He's shoving note-scrawls
and crude sketches in my face,
    dripping sweat on the canvas.

Alligators, he gasps, *anhingas*,
    last babble of a foresworn language.
I instruct him to take a breath,
    take a seat, calm down for fuck's sake.

I close my book, raise damp pages
    and a bolt of good whiskey.
I know where this is going and sigh.
    Flip a couple of sheets, glance

at the primitive iterations, and,
    gentleman that I am, unfold
the terrain map for a cursory look.
    Crocodiles, I say, *cormorants*.

His eyes go wide as the valueless
    coins of this country's currency.
B-but . . ., he begins. I interrupt:
    Crocodiles. Cormorants. Sorry.

I return his limp pad, order him
    to load carbs and prunes, hydrate,
hit the shower, hit the hay, tomorrow
    another et cetera and so forth.

He slumps out, wordless, dragging
    a backpack. When he's gone,
I replenish my ice. Maybe in time
    the kid'll catch on. Maybe not.

Ode to the Leaf-Cutting Ants
of Costa Rica

You may recall their society
consists entirely of females, or that only
the enormous queen, resting deep in the earth
where their pristine pathways
end, is fertile. Thus, the millions are sisters.
Day and night, columns pass, shards

and angles of green hefted upward,
scissored from plants they were born to destroy.
You may applaud their industry, admire
the communal faith, perhaps have read that leaves
and stems, chewed to compost
in huge subterranean galleries,

cultivate a bread-like fungus, its fruiting bodies
sustenance for all. The girls are mushroom
farmers! Diligent, entrepreneurial,
tireless, selfless, nameless. But all that you know.
What's important is they are company to a man.
To bring out a chair at dusk, to study

the frantic labor of their small, exerted lives.
To speak to them—*¿por que no?*—
as clouds congress, as sparks of houses
dot hill and valley. Bravo! Good work! And as to
a fierce caste system of minors, workers,
ferocious guards? Such, you shrug, is the world.

At least it's family. Including her there,
clutching in jaws a gigantic purple bloom
of verbena, ten times the size of the body,
reeling in tipsy, endearing circles
far from the orderly path. Look. There
she goes, almost over the edge, then careening

back with her bright bounty, a zigzag
further yet from the rest. The poet of the brood,
or perhaps the dim one. Where's she going?
She doesn't care one bit. She'll get there.

Iguana

A hard lesson to fully accept:
    That the wild blessing will appear
        only when you cease
            to hunt it, only when effort

is abandoned and, vanquished,
    you are thinking other thoughts—
        of home, perhaps, or a regret
            unforgiven. I am outside my door,

taking therapy of heat and wind.
    Five hot hours by bus, brutal
        trekking of jungle and beach
            in search of the great lizard. Nothing.

Now returned, I look up from reverie
    and it is posed for appraisal,
        emerged from iron bars of grating,
            armor gleaming in the sun.

Fleshy neck extended and an eye
    turned to me. Friend, you doubt
        my conceit, the drum lately
            sounded, that if I sit humbly

the world will come and look?
    We consider each other, patient,
        testing. I feel the old happiness,
            chase the beast into retreat and return

to my chair. Moments later,
    a reptilian head reappears
        above bars, huge crooked claws emerge,
            serrated ridge of thick tail.

We do this again, and again,
    pass hours in parry and play.
        I tell you, my squamous friend
            had no wish to be elsewhere,

that it needed some company
this lonely holiday morning.
I tell you it couldn't get enough
of my monstrous, alien beauty!

Turkey Vulture

The trees ached with *now*,
with *more*, the leaves frantic
with *again, again.* I sat
listening, waiting, and the dark wings
passed before the window,
massive and sudden, arcing
into branches, shadow
delineating shadow.
The horrible bird circled and passed again,
and then another joined its
greedy search party,
flexing and eddying
on the wind, and this was
the world, the undulating
awful immediacy,
long wings enveloping,
implausible in their gracefulness,
easy in their power,
as relentless
it passed a third time
before me and I answered,
stumbling from my shelter,
tearily scanning the sun, laughing.

There, perched high and isolate,
the thick, ashen bulk of the body,
diminutive crimson head,
spectre nourished
on a diet of death, and the sky
roaring and the sweet
chaos of the decades' song, to have been
of this raw abundance,
this immaculate unceasing
and even now present—
defeated, joyful, heart surging
and eye to eye with the scavenger-
god, whatever remained
for me, however many days more,
even just this one,
would be enough.

The Sea's Argument and After

If I swore to you that the first night,
then each subsequent, the sea crashed
her gavel onto stones diminished
to a verdict of sand, that the first night
and each subsequent she entreated me
and me alone, so finally I opened the flap
of a trembling tent and, dressed only in shorts,
descended the muddy slope of edges
and darkness to answer her, if I swore this
on my remaining life you would
smile and shake your head, recalling
how I am, believing me a little crazy only if
I really meant it. Go ahead. I meant it.
One couldn't sleep, anyway, hovering on a cot,
supplicant in lightless time and space.
Her cooing roar, her ceaseless thunder,
upheavals that, to a man suddenly
awake and upright in the dark, sounded
his sure, sudden end, the whole stupid hill
and its human wanderer washed away
and why not, now and here? So I went.
The black horizonless sky, the foaming white
of her argument. Enough was enough.
I screamed into the *sturm und drang* that I'd
heard it all before, the bullying options,
each battering old truth, I knew it all already.
Tell me something new, bitch, that I can use.
Okay, maybe now you're a bit worried?,
me half-naked and half-baked, you're guessing
a little drunk on cheap rum, two-fisted
and threatening the cold, wild Pacific?
Okay, worry. But if it wasn't me she addressed,
then whom? I was the one there, the one
who showed up, I and a single frantic
bat. As the jungle's night eyes watched,
she embraced me to the waist, towed me
to my knees then onto my back in a tangle
of arms and pain and curses. I slapped my way

back to my feet, stumbled out of reach.
Stood breathing heavily her salt, my blood,
as she hushed and purred, wailed and raged.

Residence Rescinded

Take your monkey skull
and meditations of Marcus Aurelius,
the wool socks you never wore
and the umbrella unopened.

Take your bird book
and notations, binoculars
and a single, secret letter
better pledged to a struck match

but you just couldn't. Take your drift-
wood contraband, cards for solitaire,
what's left in the bottle. Take
the alarm clock, take the snacks,

take what valueless coins remain,
a bulging sackful
to barely get you out of here.
Take your taxi driver repartee,

stutter-steps of language,
breaststrokes to enrage the pool.
Take your blueprints and mortgage
specs for beach development,

your very special opportunity
and guaranteed return,
take the aboriginal chocolates.
Take your debates with the moon,

your fistfights with the wind
you judged a draw, your bones saved
for the stinking local dogs.
Take the photograph from the icebox

door, take the magnet.
Take the number of the man to call.
Take the state papers that name you.
Take your receipts for what it

cost, all of it, everything. Take your
fucking dreams of conquest
and kindness. Kindly take every trace.
The same song banged out

for a hundred days and deaf nights,
for our benefit. Yes, you've
entertained enough with how much
we've still to learn. If you had any,

it would be part of your charm.

Advent Devotion for the Actual World

—Isaiah 11:6–9, author's translation

The wolf will feast on the bleating lamb,
the leopard on the goat, freshly gutted.
And the lion, in play with calf and yearling,
enact his teasing slaughter,
and the child find its way along
the road of bones for signs and sustenance.

The ox will stuff the bear's belly,
and of the young of their rutting, lain together,
the bear will also eat her fill,
and the jackal, ever maddened for flesh,
will piss on the straw of the kine.

The infant will rest in the cobra's den,
be solaced by him, and this child,
born to a bold vision, will thrust its hand
into the viper's nest and be rewarded
with its venom.

And your Holy Mountain
will burn, descended upon by every league
of creature, all led against you
by the wild-eyed child, feverish and laughing.
And the earth will flood, indeed,
with the tidal knowledge of the Lord
it was made to bow to, the Lord it craved.

And the crow will watch over it all
and, at the end, will sing.

Biographical Note

Gaylord Brewer is author of 15 books of poetry, fiction, creative nonfiction, and literary criticism, including *Charles Bukowski* (Macmillan, 1997), the novella *Octavius the 1st* (Red Hen, 2008), the poetry collection *Country of Ghost* (Red Hen, 2015), and the cookbook-memoir *The Poet's Guide to Food, Drink, & Desire* (Stephen F. Austin, 2015). *The Feral Condition* is his 10th volume of poetry. 1,000 individual poems have been published in journals and anthologies, including *The Bedford Introduction to Literature* and *Best American Poetry*.

Brewer was awarded a Tennessee Arts Commission Individual Artist Fellowship in 2009. He has had numerous international writing residencies—including Hawthornden Castle (Scotland), the Fundación Valparaíso (Spain), and the Global Arts Village (India)—and has taught in Russia, Kenya, England, and the Czech Republic. He earned a Ph.D. from Ohio State University and has been a member of the Middle Tennessee State University Department of English since 1993.